The Dog

Loyal Companion

Valérie Tracqui

Photos by Marie-Luce Hubert
and Jean-Louis Klein of the BIOS Agency

 Charlesbridge

Friendship

A dog learns to understand its owner's wishes by watching hand gestures and listening to commands. Holding a hand up and saying, "Stay," will let a dog know that it must wait patiently for its owner to return.

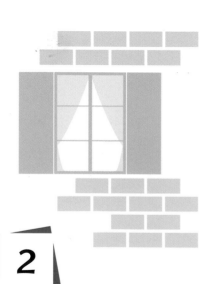

Dogs like to join in family activities and chores.

This dog understands that he's supposed to stay home.

A dog will be happy as long as it is not left alone for too long. Dogs are social animals, and they need people around to pet them and talk to them during the day.

3

It is easy to recognize a dog's tracks. They show four toes tipped with claws. The dog's fifth toe is too high on its foot to leave a mark on the ground.

Sometimes a dog will dig a hole so big that its head disappears inside. Moles and field mice had better beware!

Dogs have excellent hearing. At the slightest sound, a dog perks up its ears and turns or cocks its head to locate the sound.

Following commands

This dog is a golden retriever. Retrievers love to explore new places. If a retriever smells a mole, it freezes in place until it locates the scent. Then it bounds forward and digs excitedly with its front paws. If its owner calls, the dog stops immediately and returns to its owner's side.

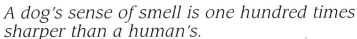 *A dog's sense of smell is one hundred times sharper than a human's.*

Time for a walk

Most dogs enjoy going for a walk. A dog holds its tail up high or wags it to show happiness and excitement. Depending on the commands, it runs or comes back to heel. Heeling means the dog must walk right next to its owner's feet.

A dog's owner uses a combination of words and gestures to tell the dog what to do.

Most golden retrievers love the water. The dog's thick undercoat helps keep its skin dry, protecting the retriever from getting too cold.

 The retriever is an excellent swimmer. It can even dive about six feet below the surface.

A retriever's favorite game is fetch. It will chase a ball for hours, picking it up in its jaws and bringing it back time after time. Dog owners should praise their dog every time it returns so that the dog will know it has performed well.

 "Retriever" means one that fetches things. These dogs live up to their name by fetching a toy from the water.

7

Sometimes thorns get stuck in a dog's paws. The dog's owner must take them out.

Dog food combines meat, vegetables, and minerals.

This dog is curled up in its basket with its playmate—a cat. They are friends because they grew up together.

It is important to brush your dog's fur to keep it healthy and shiny.

Home again

When a dog comes out of the water, it shakes itself from head to toe to get rid of the water in its fur. The dog's owner should brush out any mud and tangles with a dog brush or comb. Most dogs stretch out to enjoy the attention. To say thank you, a dog licks its owner's hand. Once the dog eats its supper it lies down to rest happily.

In the city

A dog must obey a lot of rules when it is in a city. A dog must be on a leash, and it should not pull or try to walk faster than its owner. Sometimes a dog urinates on lampposts and mailboxes. It wants other dogs to know that it passed by that area. A city street is full of distractions and dangers, so a good dog must pay careful attention to its owner.

This dog's owner scolds it by grabbing the loose fur on the dog's neck, just like its mother used to when it was a puppy.

🐾 A male dog lifts its leg to urinate, but a female just squats on her hind legs.

🐾 This dog knows it must wait quietly for its owner.

🐾 Many dogs like to ride in a car or a truck. When it is hot outside, the dog opens its mouth and pants. Sweat forms on the pads of its feet.

The male, on the left, is bigger and heavier than the female and also has longer hair.

Puppy love

Twice a year, female dogs go into heat, which means they are ready to mate. A male dog gets excited when he smells a female in heat. He follows her around until she allows him to mate with her. For two months, the puppies grow inside their mother's tummy. Soon the mother's nipples swell with milk. It is almost time to give birth.

 At first, puppies sleep all the time and should not be handled. They wake up only when they get hungry.

Puppies drink their mother's milk until they are about six or seven weeks old.

This puppy is curious about everything. There is so much to learn!

A special day

One by one, the puppies are born head first. The puppies are born blind and deaf, but they know how to find their mother's milk. They start to hear when they are fifteen days old, and they will take their first steps when they are about three weeks old. At about four or five weeks, a puppy's sight is well developed. Their first teeth, called milk teeth, come in quickly.

When puppies are separated from their mother at about two months old, they comfort themselves with a stuffed toy.

15

Playtime

A puppy learns by playing games. For two months, it memorizes every new discovery: strange noises, crying babies, older people who walk with canes, other animals. . . . The puppy learns not to be afraid of new people and experiences. It learns not to bite and to wait patiently for its meals.

16

A puppy always tests its new owner when it is adopted. It needs to find its place in its new family, and the puppy wants to be in charge.

To test its strength, the puppy jumps and pulls, bites and plays.

Dogs like to wrestle. It is just for fun, though, and no one gets hurt.

The dog that ends up on top is the winner.

This young dog obeys her owner because she likes to be rewarded and praised. Soon, she will be as well behaved as her father.

Almost grown

All young dogs love to play and act silly, but if an owner is patient and rewards the dog every time it obeys, it will quickly learn to behave. By the time a dog is three or four months old, it is usually housebroken and can obey basic commands such as come, sit, stay, and lie down—even if the dog would rather play fetch or hide-and-seek!

A puppy needs a lot of toys. If it can't find any, it might take a slipper instead!

A puppy's milk teeth fall out when the puppy is between three and six months old. Adult teeth grow in to replace them.

Best friends

After a few years, a dog and its owner become best friends. The dog understands its owner's commands immediately, and the owner knows how the dog is feeling by the expression on its face and by the way it holds its tail and ears. A well-trained dog is welcome almost everywhere. It is the best friend a person could have.

You can win a dog's loyalty by talking to it gently and showing it that even though you are in charge, you love it and will always take care of it.

21

An old partnership

At least twelve thousand years ago, people were already living with dogs and their close cousins the wolves. We still use the strength, intelligence, and keen sense of smell of some dog breeds to help us do many different things.

 This golden retriever is trained to help disabled children.

Working dogs

A dog is one of the best medicines for depression, sadness, and loneliness. Some dogs work with people who are blind or in wheelchairs. Labrador and golden retrievers are known to be gentle, polite dogs that enjoy working hard to please their owners. These dogs can learn more than thirty different commands to help them in their work.

Special training

Sled dogs can pull heavy loads across all kinds of terrain. Sheepdogs help shepherds control their flocks. Some dogs use their keen sense of smell to find lost people or items. All dogs enjoy playing sports with their owners. For example, an obstacle course is a great game. The owner shouts commands and praise while the dog jumps hedges, squirms through tunnels, and climbs up beams.

Each sled dog knows its place, and the dogs all work together to pull the sled.

Lifesavers

The German shepherd's sense of smell is so good that these dogs are often sent to find lost or injured people in landslides or avalanches. Another breed known for its daring rescues is the Saint Bernard. These large mountain dogs find lost people in snow and fog. Over the years, dogs have saved many people's lives.

This dog is being lowered into a cave to help find an injured person.

23

Dog breeds

Dogs come in all shapes, sizes, and colors. Although they all belong to the same species, each kind of dog is a different breed, and each breed has its own personality, qualities, and faults. Sheepdogs, hunting dogs, guard dogs, and family dogs are carefully chosen depending on their breed's reputation.

The **Pyrenean sheepdog** is not afraid of hard work or rain. A tough mountain dog, it guards and herds sheep, following orders from its owner.

The **Brittany** is a great hunting dog. It has a very strong sense of smell. As soon as it smells a rabbit or partridge, it freezes in place with its paw raised and points for its owner. The Brittany is also very brave and loyal.

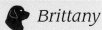 *Brittany*

24

The **Yorkshire terrier** sometimes looks like a dressed-up, overgrown toy, but it is really an excellent rat hunter that loves to run and run. It may look adorable, but the Yorkshire terrier is not just a cuddly lapdog.

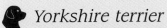
Yorkshire terrier

Great Dane

The **Great Dane** is very big and strong. It is a friendly and outgoing dog that enjoys being near its owner. The Great Dane is also a wonderful guard dog when properly trained.

The **bichon frise** is a lapdog that is playful and affectionate. It also enjoys running and jumping very high like the poodle.

bichon frise

25

A Quick Quiz about the Dog:

Photograph credits:
BIOS Agency: All photographs by J.-L. Klein and M.-L. Hubert/Bios except: www.corbis.com/CORBIS: p. 2-3; J.-M. Cresto: p. 4 (top right); Kent and Donna Dannen c/o Mira: p. 7 (bottom); W. Meinderts/Fotonatura: p. 8-9 (bottom); M. Bruno: p. 14 (bottom left); J.-L. and F. Ziegler: p. 22-23 (top), p. 23 (bottom).
F. Reinhart/Anecah: p. 22 (bottom); E. Baccega/Colibri: p. 25 (top right)